The
ONE M1NUTE
NETWORKER™

*The nine simple laws of networking
that will change your life forever.*

BRYAN THAYER

The One Minute Networker

Printed in the United States of America

ISBN 0-9672098-1-1

Acknowledgements

While this book is the culmination of my experiences and interviews with many, many networkers, special thanks for their individual contributions goes to Jim Lindle, Richard Brooke, Robert Butwin, Bob Snyder, Bruce Call, Mindy Jones, Dean Naylor, Drew Earl, Duncan MacDonald, Mitch Huhem, Mark Ludwig and Mike McDonald. Friends who reviewed the manuscript and provided valuable feedback include Jackie Thayer, Alan Peterson, Beau Tolman, Ricky Hatch, Kerri Scarbrough and Mark Ishii.

Writing a book is not a simple task, especially when there is a company to run and family responsibilities at the same time. I need to acknowledge the assistance of Rod Clifford in the creation of The One Minute Networker. A writer with expertise in organization communications, his help is much appreciated.

The Nine Laws of Networking

Networking isn't only something you do, It's something you let happen to you.

Introduction

Several years ago in my office I was visiting with a very successful businessman and investor, a man who is worth millions. As we got up to go to lunch, he asked if he could first quickly check some of his stocks. I started to move around my desk to give him access to my computer, but he waved me back to my chair. He said he would tell me how to log in to his account and then give me the stock symbols he wanted to check.

As I typed in each symbol he would look at the screen to track the number of shares traded, as well as the "bid" and "ask" prices. I watched as he carefully analyzed the graph indicators to decide when to get in and when to get out.

You can imagine what I was thinking - I felt like Donald Trump's chauffer listening in on his phone calls. This was very valuable information. This man had made millions using the very kind of information I was watching him review. What might I have been able to do with that information? I wanted to record everything I was seeing, but for the sake of the relationship I didn't.

While the opportunity to watch him work was purely coincidental, my business has required me to interview more than a thousand top performers just like him specifically to learn what makes them successful in their respective fields. These are men and women from all over the world who have achieved some amazing lifestyles.

Since 1989, I have been in the multi-media production business. My company helps successful businesses move to the next level. We develop marketing tools that help them sell themselves and their products. We give them the ability to communicate more effectively to their various audiences. To do that, we first have to know the people behind the company and what makes them tick.

Now I want to tell you what I've observed about those incredibly successful people. They aren't necessarily highly educated or unusually talented. For the most part they are pretty ordinary people who are accomplishing extraordinary things simply by capitalizing on the resources of their personal networks. And something else that's very important - they come in all ages. None of them ever believed that they were too young or too old to change their lives and achieve their dreams! That's the message I want to share.

In the following chapters you'll learn the principles behind those achievements; principles you can apply in your own personal and business life. Most important, you'll come to understand that you have a network of your own, with all of the resources you need to succeed.

After all these years, I firmly believe that any of us can reach our goals and dreams if we'll just relax and let success happen to us. Here's how.

EVEN THE SMALLEST MOTION CAN MULTIPLY INTO A DRIVING FORCE

LAW #1
Networking Happens

An old Vietnamese folk tale speaks of a man named Mr. Straw, a kind and generous man who was very poor. He owned nothing more than the clothes he wore, but he believed in being thoughtful and considerate of others. One day while Mr. Straw was praying at the temple, he heard a voice that said, "When you leave the temple steps the first thing you touch will bring you wealth."

He didn't know what to think. Would he pick up a stone that turned out to be a diamond? Would he touch a brick and have it magically turn to gold? Had he heard the voice correctly? Had he even heard a voice at all?

As he left the temple and walked down the steps, Mr. Straw was so deep in thought that he lost his footing and fell sprawling into the dust. When he picked himself up, he found that during the fall his hand had grasped a piece of straw. Normally he would have cast it aside. But he

remembered the voice in the temple telling him that the
first thing he touched would bring wealth. So, clutching
that piece of straw, he began his journey home.

As he walked, a dragonfly began buzzing around him.
No amount of shooing could get the insect to fly away. So
Mr. Straw caught the dragonfly and tied it to the piece of
straw so that it looked like a little kite. Then he continued
down the road.

Soon he met a flower lady coming from the other
direction. She had her young son with her, and the boy was
very weary. He had risen early to go sell flowers with his
mother, and now the day was hot and the road dusty. But as
soon as he saw the dragonfly tied to the straw, his eyes lit up.

"What a wonderful pet!" the boy exclaimed. Now, Mr.
Straw knew that the voice in the temple had said the straw
would bring him wealth, but the boy was tired and this simple
dragonfly brought him such joy. Mr. Straw handed the little
contraption to the boy. The flower lady was so grateful that
she gave Mr. Straw the last flower she had, a beautiful rose.

As Mr. Straw continued his journey, he chanced upon a
young man sitting forlornly under a tree. "Why are you so
sad?" Mr. Straw asked. "Today I will ask my beloved to
marry me," replied the young man. "But I have no gift for
her that can match her beauty."

"All I have is this rose," replied Mr. Straw. "But it is a beautiful rose, and you are welcome to it."

The young man was overjoyed at the stranger's generosity, and in exchange he gave Mr. Straw three plump, juicy oranges that he had carried for his lunch. Soon after this encounter, Mr. Straw came upon a peddler pulling his cart through the choking dust of the road.

"Can you help me?" asked the peddler. "I am without water and am very thirsty."

"I'm sorry," replied Mr. Straw, "I have no water. But you can have these oranges. They are very large and the juice from them will quench your thirst."

The peddler gratefully accepted the oranges and pulled a bolt of silk from his cart, which he gave to Mr. Straw as a token of his appreciation. Several miles later, as Mr. Straw entered town with a bolt of beautiful silk under his arm, a princess in a golden carriage stopped him.

"Where did you get that silk?" asked the princess. "It is my father's birthday, and I have looked in every shop for silk exactly like that to make my father a new robe. Tell me where you found such exquisite material, and I will go there immediately."

"I do not know which shop this silk came from," said Mr. Straw. "But since it is your father's birthday, please take this bolt of silk as a gift from me."

Overjoyed at the man's generosity, the princess accepted the silk, but only if Mr. Straw would accept a jewel in return. After the princess was on her way, he looked at the jewel that shone like the sun. The voice in the temple had been right. Mr. Straw sold the jewel and with the money he received he bought a great rice field. He worked the field year after year, becoming a wealthy man.

But his wealth did not change Mr. Straw. He still always shared rice with the hungry. He built a school for the children in his village and he helped those who were in need.

This tale has been handed down from generation to generation to teach kindness. In the story it is not the piece of straw that begins the chain of events leading to wealth for Mr. Straw. It is his kindness toward others. Mr. Straw's wealth came as a natural result, not of calculated investments and business deals, but of who he was and how he reacted to those he met during the course of his regular routine. You, too, can reach a point that your own success will result from who you are, what you do every day and those with whom you connect along the way.

Several years ago it became popular to play a little mind game called "Six Degrees to Kevin Bacon." It was based loosely on the theory of social scientist Stanley Milgram that all of the world's people are connected to each other by no more than six degrees of separation, or six sets of acquaintances. Now the fate of the world doesn't actually depend on anyone connecting to Kevin Bacon, but the whole idea of "connectedness" has intrigued me for a long time.

It is one of the identifiable characteristics common to every successful person I've met. Each of them is connected in various ways to literally thousands of others. It is through those connections - a network - that they have built their success. If they can, you can.

Proof of that is what you have already done. If you could push the "rewind" button on your life you would find that just about every important decision you made or opportunity that came your way was influenced by someone you knew and trusted, someone to whom you were connected in some way.

Chances are that you're in a business or a career that you're trying to grow, but are unsure how to do that. Maybe you've listened to a big-name motivational speaker and came away thinking, "Who am I kidding? My personality is nothing like that." Or you investigated a business opportunity and were far short of the required investment. So what now? Do you have to contort yourself into some kind of high-powered sales personality that isn't really you? Do you have to somehow find a large amount of start-up capital before you can succeed?

> **Networking isn't only something you do, It's something you let happen to you.**

Well, no, you don't have to do either. It's not necessary to change who you are; you don't need a personality transplant or a huge bank account. Just do the things you regularly do throughout your day — every day - use the existing connections in your network, and create new ones. Become a committed networker!

One of the largest living organisms in the world is a grove of aspen trees. The aspen tree reproduces by sending out "shoots" from its root system. A shoot is simply a horizontally growing stem or root that grows out some distance from the parent plant and takes root, forming a new plant. It is estimated that this unique aspen grove contains more than 41,000 trees, all of them ultimately linked back to a single original tree. They're networked; their root systems are connected. Each tree flourishes because all of the others flourish.

Like the aspen tree, you send out shoots every day that connect you to other people, including some you don't even know yet. Literally, since the day you were born you have been building an amazingly powerful network of relationships. Some of those relationships, of course, are family members and friends. But your network also includes former teachers, co-workers, neighbors, clergy, casual acquaintances, customers, your insurance agent, the person who takes your dry cleaning - virtually everyone you deal with on some level, whether it's every day, once a week or once a year. You already use this network often.

For example, when your car needs repair, you probably don't look up a mechanic in the phone book. You take the vehicle to a mechanic who has been recommended by a friend or someone else you trust. The same thing is true of your hair stylist or nail technician. If you should build a new home, you're likely to use a contractor whose work is recommended by someone you know. This list can go on and on, and each of us has one. This network is your personal life support system, and you're already comfortable using it. The more you use it the more useful the network becomes.

Now all you have to do is learn to use your network more effectively, not simply to get your car tuned up and running smoothly, but to get your life tuned up and running smoothly. I said earlier in this chapter that you don't need a huge bank account. That's because, as you effectively utilize all of the connections you already have, you'll realize that your network is your working capital - and there's no credit limit! As you begin to wield the power of your personal network you'll come to understand that your net worth is the product of your network.

When you think about it, networking couldn't be simpler. You just act on a natural impulse to help someone else, and graciously accept help when it's offered. Fortunately it doesn't require a disaster of some sort or imminent danger to move us to help others. It's only necessary that we take note of life happening around us. My friend, Dean Naylor, brought more than two million new customers to Sprint by being observant of others' needs. "Life leaves clues!" he advises. "Pay attention."

Technology has made it possible to make contacts without personal connections. We can contact almost anyone anywhere in the world without having to actually make a personal connection with another individual. Real conversation is too easily replaced by the diversion of 200+ cable television channels, literally millions of Internet sites, video games on cell phones, e-mail, etc. It's estimated that the average amount of time American parents and their children spend talking to each other every day is as little as 15 minutes! As a result, studies now tell us that people, especially children, increasingly are feeling isolated and alone in the world. What a great opportunity for you to connect with those who need to feel connected but aren't! There's never been a more perfect time to reconnect with and expand your network, personally and professionally.

For example, perhaps you notice that the neighbor down the block seems to be home every day. Has he lost his job? If so, can you or someone in your network help him? Maybe. At back-to-school night you visit with the owner of a popular boutique and learn that she's having difficulty finding a reliable employee. Do you know someone who is perfect for that position? If not, do you know someone who knows someone who can help her? You probably do. You get a phone call one day from someone who says, "A friend of mine gave me your name. He met you at a Little League game and..." All of these are clues that opportunity is knocking. Are you listening? Are you paying attention?

The next time you happen to think of an old friend you've not seen in a long time, or a memory flashes in your mind of someone in your past, do something about it. Pick up the phone and call that person, or scribble a note right away. There's probably a good reason why you thought about that individual. Opportunity doesn't like loose ends; it's always trying to connect us with others and complete the web.

So don't put it off when someone's name pops into your mind. This takes some personal discipline because it's too easy to say, "I'll call later" or "I'm busy right now." Just do it now. Renew those friendships; refresh that network, make those connections. When you do that, your view of those individuals changes. You have moved them from memory to the present. And those people now see you as someone who is interested in them. They're now in your corner when you need them.

One of my best friends is my high school teacher, Don Ward. He taught Advanced Placement History, and every student who took his class had a 93% chance of passing the AP exam for college credit. Don knew every student's name.

People like Don are increasingly rare. At least once during each of the last 20 years Don has stopped by to say hello. We catch up on his family, my family, some of my high school classmates he has seen recently. Then as suddenly as he arrives, he's gone. But after he leaves I feel great. The interesting thing about Don is that literally hundreds of his former students feel the same way. Think of all the people and resources he has available in his network, thousands of students who moved on into careers, businesses and professions.

To begin understanding your personal network, make a list containing at least 25 names from that network. These should be people, like Don Ward, who have positively influenced you and others in some way, individuals who bring a smile to your face when you think of them.

Being an effective networker doesn't take much time at all; never more than a minute or so. Life happens one minute at a time. So does networking. After you've made the principles in the following chapters part of your life, you'll use those minutes effectively by letting networking happen! Remember: Network = Net Worth. Become a One Minute Networker!

THE MOMENT ONE COMMITS ONESELF,
THEN PROVIDENCE MOVES, TOO.

– JOHAN VON GOETHE

LAW #2
Scarcity vs. Abundance

I was financially successful at an age when most men and women are still just starting a career. A number of factors came together at the right time and I found myself earning a lot of money. I bought a beautiful house, drove expensive cars, traveled with my wife and generally lived the good life.

Then one summer my brother-in-law and his wife came to visit. As we sat talking one night, his wife looked around the large living room and said, "What if something goes wrong? How can you keep all of this up?" She asked innocently enough, but she had struck a chord.

Later that night after everyone was in bed and it was quiet in the house, I stood at the huge window overlooking the city below, reviewing in my mind all of the things I possessed. The sheer size of the room, with its cathedral ceiling and tall windows, made me feel small. Suddenly the thought came to me, "What am I doing here? What if I really can't keep this up? What then?" Suddenly I was terrified.

Without realizing it, despite the physical abundance all around me, I had slipped into scarcity. My confidence was shaken. As a result, things began to go badly in my business. In fact, I got into a business venture that was outside my area of expertise and lost my investment. I made an unwise real estate purchase that went south. Eventually we sold the house and significantly moderated our lifestyle.

It wasn't until I began living in abundance again - acknowledging blessings and recognizing opportunities — that everything improved. I decided to get back on track. I rented a tiny office containing nothing but a desk and a telephone. One day, out of the blue, a man I'd briefly met once called to offer me an ownership position in his company. I barely remembered him. We had been introduced a couple of years earlier by a mutual friend and that was that. But now, he had somehow heard about my earlier accomplishments and my abilities fit his needs at that time.

It was a turning point, not because of the offer itself, but because I suddenly felt again that I had something to contribute, that someone needed my skills and abilities. That realization began my transition from scarcity to abundance, even though at the end of my phone call with him nothing had yet changed financially. But everything had changed in my head, in my attitude. I only worked

there for a month - a successful month - before I decided
that job was not how I wanted to earn a living.

But because my attitude and my confidence had
changed, I was able to go back to that little office and turn
things around. By living in abundance again I began to
expect things to get better - and they did. That "out of the
blue" phone call made a huge difference for me when I most
needed it. I'll bet there is someone in your network who
could use a confidence-building phone call like that one.

Pause right now and, in the margin of this page, write
the first name that comes to mind. Send that person a card
or call him or her - just out of the blue. No strings attached.
Simply give a compliment about something you appreciate
about them.

Scarcity vs. Abundance has little to do with money and
everything to do with attitude. Living in scarcity means
accepting your circumstances and believing you can't
change them. You believe that what you are today is what
you will be tomorrow because there just isn't a way out.
When you worry about what you don't want to happen, you
begin to attract those very things that dull the senses to any
kind of innovative solutions to the problems.

Scarcity isn't a financial problem - though often that is a
result - as much as it is a small, narrow way of looking at life.

Those who live in scarcity cannot recognize the good things they have, such as their family, a home, friends — it's a long list. Instead they see only family problems, the mortgage, strained friendships - the downside of every good thing.

Even more important, those who live in scarcity usually live with fear: fear of failure (even if they haven't failed), fear of success (even if they are successful) and fear of the unknown. If you are one of those who fearfully live in scarcity - and there are millions who do - the things you most want in life will remain out of reach until you learn to live in abundance.

Fear is created because the human mind naturally seeks the familiar and avoids the unknown. Faced with a decision about the future, our minds go back to earlier experiences to find a reference point. Unfortunately, sometimes that reference point is a negative experience from our past. So instead of seeing all of the possibilities (living in abundance), we see only mistakes we don't want to repeat (living in scarcity).

Fear also causes procrastination. How often do we put off making a difficult phone call because we're afraid of what will happen if the person we're calling actually picks up the phone? As long as we can avoid dialing that number, find something else to do, divert our attention with less important busywork, we don't have to worry about it. Some of us are more interested in the potential than in the reality.

But not moving ahead while we comfortably remain in the past has its own set of risks. If your past includes bad experiences, dwelling on them just replays the fear movie over and over in your mind. It will pull you down until there is no difference between the remembered past and the actual present. Sometimes, in fact, we replay the past so often that our mind begins to create scenes and memories that never happened.

But if your past is full of good memories, focusing on them instead of facing today can be just as detrimental. If you're saying to yourself, "Ten years ago I was driving a better car..." or "Things were better before I..." you make it impossible to see and plan for the future.

Early in my career a new salesman came into the office, a man who had fifteen more years of experience than I did at the time. All he could talk about were the good old days. He scared me. I thought, "I don't want to be like that, where all I can do is talk about how good things used to be." There is no need to look backward. You have to take lessons from the past, but live in the present as you build your future. The future is where all the action is anyway.

Ask yourself: "Am I looking for scarcity and fear, or am I seeking abundance and joy? What am I trying to hold on to?" Others can see it, usually within seconds of meeting you. They can feel it, even over the phone. Step outside of yourself for a moment to see what image you're projecting. Introspectively asking the right questions will reveal what you're really feeling.

Generally, the people I know whose lives are constantly difficult are almost addicted to struggle. They are so used to it that if they didn't always live in crisis or confusion they actually would feel uncomfortable. If this sounds like you,

> **Abundance is a fullness of life, regardless of income.**

remember that you're creating a new negative experience every day. You'll stop having those experiences only when you change how you feel about yourself and change what you expect your life to be.

Scarcity - both the mindset and the financial reality - can cause you to focus too narrowly on meeting your immediate needs instead of more long-term security. It has a cascading effect. For example, if you have a prospect very close to doing business with you, it may be tempting to spend the money you're expecting but don't yet have. Then if the deal falls through and the paperwork is never signed, you'll have to scramble and use your energy to meet your immediate needs. You no longer have the luxury of planning your future because you're too busy trying to fix the crisis of the day.

Conversely, living in abundance means that you recognize the possibilities that are everywhere around you. You know tomorrow will be better because of what you do today. If scarcity is not a financial problem, abundance is not necessarily a financial bonanza, although it can be. Abundance is a fullness of life, regardless of income, an appreciation for the good things that come to those who see the upside of every circumstance. One of my favorite musical artists, Sting, has said it's always been his strategy in life to be optimistic. With 12 albums selling more than 100 million copies worldwide, it seems to have worked out pretty well for him.

When you live in abundance you are not governed by fear or doubt. You enjoy what many describe as blessings, understanding that you can overcome problems with your own creativity, hard work and help from those in your circle. You recognize opportunities that come to you and are not afraid to take advantage of them. If you live in abundance you can reach whatever goals you set in your life.

Living in scarcity cannot solve problems; neither can it

recognize opportunities. The One Minute Networker understands that any great opportunity is worthless if you can't afford to take it, if you're not living within your means. The law of abundance means that whether or not you sign that prospect or close that deal, your life will not change for better or worse immediately because you're prepared. There is plenty to go around, for you and for everyone else.

Living in abundance means that if you make a contact or meet a prospect who has certain needs that must be filled before they can deal with your offer, you just automatically help them first. You can do that because you're not running out of time trying to make a buck.

Speaking of making a buck, let me tell you about a man named Bucky, whose life offers the perfect contrast between scarcity and abundance. In 1927, Bucky's life was in shambles. Actually, it was worse than shambles — he was contemplating suicide. He was unemployed, bankrupt, and his reputation was ruined. His first child had died, and now he and his wife had a new baby girl to share in their misery. They could scarcely think about the trials their daughter would face.

Then Bucky began to feel that maybe he was on the brink of something big. Either good or bad, something big would happen, and soon. This premonition occupied most of his thoughts. He found himself spending hours sitting on his living room couch, almost grasping this new... new something. He couldn't reach it, couldn't understand it, but he knew it was there. And he was determined to find it.

He didn't find it overnight. He spent another year struggling to pay the bills, to buy food for the family, and to maintain some semblance of dignity as a jobless, penniless nobody. Finally, Bucky reached the breaking point.

That winter, the despondent 32-year-old man wandered through the streets of Chicago, eventually finding himself on the shores of Lake Michigan. As he looked into the icy waters, he entertained a strong urge to throw himself in — to give up and end all his pain. But before he could act on this urge, a thought entered his mind: "You do not have the right to eliminate yourself. You do not belong to you. You belong to the universe."

At that decisive moment, Bucky found what he had been seeking for the past year. He decided, "...to find what a single individual could contribute to changing the world and benefiting all humanity." He decided to have an attitude of abundance. He promised God, the Universe —whatever you choose to call it — that he would devote the rest of his life not to earning a living, but to living in a manner where he would bless as many lives as humanly possible.

Bucky's agreement was more concise than a general promise to help others. He made a specific commitment that he would take whatever money was left in his bank account at the end of each month and give it to someone, anyone, in need. He felt that if he honored this agreement, he would be blessed with contacts, friends, neighbors, even strangers, who would get money into his hands. He was to be a funnel, not a bucket. The money was to pass through him, not to him.

Bucky kept his word, and the miracles started coming. He met people on the beach who offered him temporary work. Old friends called, asking him to help with this or that, and paying him for it. He gained insights into designs of buildings, cars and civilizations. He created the geodesic dome, which is still used in great architecture all over the world.

Over the next 54 years, Bucky was awarded 25 patents, wrote 28 books, received 47 honorary doctorate degrees, received the Presidential Medal of Freedom, and circled the globe dozens of times, lecturing to millions. More than $30 million passed through his hands.

In 2004, twenty-one years after his death, the United States Postal Service honored Bucky — R. Buckminster Fuller, one of the world's premier architects — by issuing a commemorative postal stamp bearing his image. Beating fear, scarcity and even suicide, Bucky Fuller showed how to live an abundant life.

When I'm experiencing a tough time, I have to ask myself why it's happening. Is it really about the circumstances here in front of me, or is it something else that my mind is trying to connect with that's causing fear, pulling me back into scarcity. That's all my mind tries to do - find a path to run on. It doesn't know what's around the corner, so it latches onto the familiar past.

But when you live in the present, doing everything you can do to create success, and you have your eye on your goals for the future, a strange thing begins to happen. Solutions unfold almost in spite of you.

The nineteenth-century German philosopher Johan von Goethe put it this way:

"There is one elementary truth...that the moment one commits oneself, then Providence moves, too.

All sorts of things occur to help one that would never otherwise have occurred. A whole stream of events issues from the decision, raising in one's favor all manner of unforeseen incidents and meetings and material assistance, which no man could have dreamt would have come his way."

Seeing it and speaking it every day greatly increase your chances of success. Imagine it so clearly that you see yourself with it, enjoying it. Commit yourself to it. That's how you live in abundance.

The universe, God and everyone who cares about you want you to have it. I mention God here, and some might think that's inappropriate in a book about networking. Don't misunderstand; this is not a missionary tract for any faith or creed. But in all of those interviews that I mentioned earlier, and in all of my personal contacts with other networkers, I have never met one who did not profess a belief in God and a personal faith in divine help in their lives. I believe that is not coincidence.

Though a few wear it on their sleeves, most quietly call upon their faith for strength and encouragement when facing challenges and fear. By letting go of fear and by accepting the abundance they are entitled to enjoy, their networks make connections that take them to their goals. That will happen for you, too, even if you can't see it at the time.

My friend Jason Boreyko told me one day, "I believe that God would not give you the dream, or the desire in your heart, if he did not also give you the talent and abilities to make that dream come true."

On a business trip I was running late as I rented a car at the airport. The rental agent gave me the keys and pointed to a row of cars. I dashed out, hurried to the car and pressed the "unlock" button on the key ring. But the door didn't unlock. I pressed again and heard the click, with the same result. Twice more I pressed the button, twice more I heard it click, twice more the door remained locked.

Finally it occurred to me that I might be at the wrong car. Listening more carefully for the click, I discovered that the door locks on the adjacent car were jumping up and down. I was doing the correct thing - pressing the unlock button - and the correct result was happening, just in a different place than I expected.

Don't allow yourself to get discouraged by mistakenly thinking your network isn't working. Sometimes when you're doing everything right it seems things still aren't clicking. But they are - somewhere. Like me standing beside the wrong car, you have to look a little further or listen a little closer.

Sometimes we need to point ourselves in the direction of abundance instead of standing at the door of scarcity.

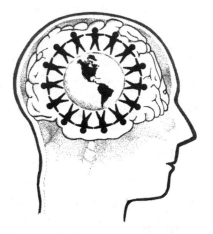

NETWORKING ISN'T MAGIC, BUT IT IS MAGICAL

LAW #3
Let Me Think What I Know

Several years ago I taught a Sunday school class of five-year-olds. One day I asked a question, and the response from most of the kids was "I don't know" or something like it. But one little girl paused and said, "Let me think what I know."

I was struck by her answer because of the lesson all of us adults could learn from it. In her innocence she didn't get all hung up on what she didn't know. She was going to look for the answer in the storehouse of things her five-year-old mind did know. She just needed to think about it first.

Your mind is constantly processing data, like a computer. Scientists tell us that we are continually taking in as much as 300 gigabytes of all kinds of information through all of our senses. But we're only conscious of about 42 gigabytes of it. Some would say that's a waste of brainpower, but successful networkers will recognize a huge potential to connect with their skills and abilities. *There is almost no limit to what the human brain can do with some training.*

For example, both President Thomas Jefferson and President James A. Garfield could write Latin with their right hand and Greek with their left hand - simultaneously! An amateur astronomer in Australia memorized - memorized — more than 1,000 star clusters! One night, while searching the heavens through his telescope, he noticed that one of those clusters "...was not right." Further investigation by astronomers led to the discovery of a supernova.

Your brain has an incredible 100 billion neurons, each of them connected to as many as eight neighboring neurons. That's more capacity than the entire World Wide Web! When you use the search engine in your head to sort through all of the information that is stored there, it can bring to your remembrance everything you've ever seen, every word you've heard, every person you've ever met. Sifting and sorting, your search engine almost automatically will piece together the answers you need.

Well, you say, that might happen with some people, like those who are already successful. But that sort of thing doesn't happen to me. That answer tells me you're living in scarcity. Now look at it with more abundant eyes. That sort of thing does, indeed, happen to you. In fact, it already has.

You've already had personal experience with it. Someone asks a question. You know the answer, but you can't think of it just now. What's your response? Probably something like, "Wait a minute, it will come to me." Or, "I'll remember when I stop thinking about it." And what happens when you stop trying to recall the answer? Your search engine noodles around in your subconscious mind, looking for it while you're on to other things. At some later time the name, date, incident - whatever you're trying to remember - suddenly pops out into your conscious thoughts.

Take a minute right now and flip back a few pages to the quote from Goethe. Focus on the phrase that says "the moment one commits oneself, then Providence moves, too." Whether you call it Providence, your subconscious mind, or something from the X-Files, this is a true principle: when you decide to act, other actions begin elsewhere that will take you to your goals. I don't know how it works; only that it does. And it will work for you as effectively as it ever has for anyone else.

In 1991 I was at a trade show where I became acquainted with a man named Walt Michaels. When I told him my company produced videos, Walt said he wasn't interested, but he knew someone who was opening a new company in Las Vegas. He gave me his business card and I wrote his contact's name and phone number on the back and put it in my wallet. Walt suggested that I call the contact "...if you get the chance."

I got the chance just a few months later when I lost my largest client. The loss of a major source of income couldn't have come at a worse time; my wife and I had just closed on a new home. If ever I needed to "think what I know", that was the time. Then almost out of nowhere I remembered Walt's card in my wallet. I made a quick call to the name on the card. For privacy reasons I'm only going to use first names here. The result of that call was a half-hour meeting with the company president, Rod. Nothing more happened at that time.

But a short time later, he called to tell me that his company was now ready to work with mine. Our relationship grew, and I was able to take advantage of some fantastic opportunities! Of course, the story doesn't stop there.

While working with Rod's company I met Jim, an extraordinarily gifted consultant based in Missouri, who was advising Rod. Jim had other clients as well, and as our working relationship grew he put me in touch with one of those clients who could use the services of my business. Jim's client became my client, resulting in more business for me. Later Jim asked if I knew anyone who could help him develop new business in Mexico.

I made some phone calls and gave him several good leads. One of those calls was to Larry, in Texas, whom I had known but not done business with. While talking with him about Jim's need for info about Mexico we began an unplanned discussion about several new projects Larry was considering. I reminded him that my company could help. He agreed, and over a short period of time Larry's business gave me several new contracts!

Now — what if I hadn't told Walt about my company way back at that trade show? What if I hadn't written his friend's name and number on the business card he gave me? What if I hadn't made that cold call to a stranger? I easily could have just ignored it and not taken either of those actions. All of the networking that came about because of the "Let me think what I know" principle ultimately was worth about $10 million!

So, who do you know? A huge number of people, that's who. And each of them knows someone else, and they all know someone... You have access to an incredible array of resources if you use this "Let me think what I know" principle. Take a minute and think of the connections you have already.

> "Insight" is just looking "inside" ourselves to see what we already know.

You'll discover that you have insight you didn't know about. After all, "insight" is just looking "inside" ourselves to see what we already know; to remember what's already there and retrieve it.

Here's another personal example. Some time ago I was getting ready to leave for a two-day conference in Baltimore.

I started my car in the driveway and, because I was running a little late, I tossed one bag onto the front seat, closed the door and went around to the other side to put in the other bag. Somehow the doors accidentally locked. There I was, the locked car was running with my bags inside! I couldn't just take another car because I would need the things in those bags at the conference.

There was a spare key, but it was 30 minutes away at my mother's house. Don't say it - I know that's a ridiculous place for a spare key. There simply wasn't enough time to go get it. If I missed the flight I'd have to wait until the next morning. By the time I could get to Baltimore the two-day conference would have been half over. I was beginning to panic, and already I was going into scarcity quickly. I should have listened to my wife, Jackie. She always says, "Don't panic until it's time to panic."

I remember putting my face in my hands, thinking, "What am I going to do?" I belong to AAA, but there was no way they could send someone to unlock my car in time to make that flight.

Then Jackie let her mind process what it already knew subconsciously about the problem. She remembered that the man we bought our house from was a policeman. So she suggested that I call him (thinking in abundance). My first thought was that the odds of him being in the area -

even if I could get reach him - were almost impossible (thinking in scarcity).

I called anyway, knowing it was useless. Guess what? He was only five minutes away; he said he would be right there. He arrived right on time, did his thing with the wire in the window and the door was opened. I made my flight, went to the conference and had a very productive experience there that generated a quarter of a million dollars. That was made possible because Jackie calmly let her mind process what she already knew until an answer appeared.

In the movie "Sabrina" Harrison Ford's character, Linus, is watching Sabrina, played by Julia Ormond, take photographs of the view from some exclusive waterfront property. He sees the way she looks for the shot; how she frames the subject. After a few minutes he asks how long she has been a photographer. Her response is classic: "Every time I look through the camera I'm surprised. It's like finding yourself in the middle of the story. I think I've been taking pictures all my life - long before I had a camera."

Like Sabrina, you have been taking pictures since the day you were born. You have imagined yourself in those pictures. Now it's time to look through your life's photo album and relive the positive sights, sounds and emotions that help you make decisions and connect with others. Today is the culmination of your lifetime of experiences that can help you

solve any problem. Use it to your advantage. Like the little
girl in my Sunday school class, stop and think what you know.

There is another positive aspect to "Let me think what I
know" as well. In the first example, Walt had nothing to gain
by referring me to Rod. He referred me anyway. I had nothing
to gain by calling Larry for Jim's benefit. I called Larry anyway.
Rod, Jim and Larry were in different parts of the country
working different businesses. There was no logical reason for
us all to connect, but we did. As I said earlier, networking
happens to you. It's not magic, but it is magical!

Whenever you meet someone new, information flows
both directions. You become acquainted with someone who
has a talent or a skill you can use sometime in the future. But
that individual also becomes acquainted with you and your
skills. Somewhere down the line, without your knowledge
and without having to do anything at all, that person will
say, "I know someone who..." - and you'll be that someone!

By being "out there" minute-by-minute you are
positioning yourself to take advantage of opportunities that
come along. Do the right thing for those in your network
whenever you can and good things will come back.

But you can't "think what I know" if your brain and your
life are cluttered with extraneous noise. It's like trying to
think of the melody of a song while another song is playing
on the radio. You can't do it. The loudest sound wins every
time, and I'm not referring only to music. All kinds of

distractions literally force themselves on our time, energy and attention every day.

I know of a prominent businessman whose entire life was marked by long hours at work, followed by more time participating in a professional association, various community and civic groups. He held responsible lay positions in his church, and of course, spent as much time as possible with his family. Some time ago he said he had reached a point that he had "...grown weary of the noise of the world."

He is now clearing away all of the unnecessary background noise in his life, focusing on more important things. Why should the rest of us wait until we're retired to do the same kind of noise-suppression in our own lives?

Try this. Make a list of two distractions you will eliminate this very week so you can hear opportunity when it knocks. A couple of examples might be TV viewing and cell phone use.

You're not likely to have any great business or career building ideas while watching Days of Our Lives or Jeopardy. It's an unnecessary and unproductive distraction. It's been estimated that the average American spends 52 full days each year watching television! No, I'm not an anti-TV fanatic. Keep your television; just cut down on the hours and make better use of your time.

Keep your cell phone, too. But there are times when a phone call is distracting. Decide when you can turn it off and then - turn it off!

YOU CAN'T SAY THE WRONG THING TO THE RIGHT PERSON

LAW #4
Working the Circle

A friend and I and our families were on our way to
vacation at Lake Powell in the gorgeous Four Corners area of
Arizona. We were in my friend's luxury motor home,
practically a hotel on wheels with lots of sleeping space, a
shower, toilet, refrigerator and microwave. It had everything.

Near the tiny town of Hanksville, in the middle of the
night, we had a flat tire on the motor home. That's when we
discovered that it wasn't equipped with quite everything. It
didn't have a spare tire. Not that it would have mattered; it
didn't have a complete jack to change a flat, either. We were
stuck in the middle of nowhere in the dark.

So I started to "work the circle" to see what I could find.
Now, I don't know how I knew this next part, but I knew it.
My friend Steve's name came to mind. He had a friend,
Aaron, who was dating a young woman, Jennie, whose
father lived in Hanksville (the four degrees of separation
didn't get me to Kevin Bacon, but it did solve my problem).

I wandered around in the desert until I found a spot where my cell phone lit up with a clear signal, and then I called Steve and explained the problem. He said, "Let me check. I'll call you right back"

I knew everyone else was thinking, "Yeah, right, Bryan. What are the chances that this is going to work?" Then Steve called back with the phone number for Jennie's dad. Within 45 minutes of my call to him, Carl Hunt arrived in a tow truck, hooked up the motor home and towed us into Hanksville.

We spent the night there, and the next morning Carl got on the phone and located a new motor home tire from a supplier he knew. (Now I'm plugged into his circle, as well as my own.) Carl even let us use his truck to go get the tire.

Finally we were back on the road, headed for our vacation spot and enjoying some really great homemade salsa Carl's wife had given us. What could have been a real disaster was averted simply because working my circle paid off in a big way that night.

Everyone understands the terms "circle of friends" and "circle of influence". But there is another one we often don't recognize. It's the huge circle of everyone we've ever known, plus all of the people they know. Because we don't have regular contact with most of them for various reasons, we don't think of them in that "circle of friends" way. But as a One Minute Networker, you'll understand the value of this vast circle - this network— and know how to work it to your advantage.

Maybe you've never been stranded at the side of the road like we were, but there have been times when you have been stuck in some other way. How did you solve the problem? Who did you call? We all have had experiences like this, large and small, when solutions came about because of our circle, our network.

Working the circle can bring us financial or business opportunities, help in a crisis, or even peace of mind when we need it. It really is nothing more than identifying people we know who have the skills or resources to help us achieve our own goals (and sometimes get us out of trouble). Many people are ready to help you grow your business and realize your dreams. It is within your network of relationships that everything good begins. Whatever venture you're in, once you tap into your network, things will begin to change.

If you think you don't know anyone who can help you get from Point A to Point B, think again. In fact, you know someone right now who can and will help you. That's true of just about anything you want or need. It is a very rare person who isn't flattered when someone, even a stranger, asks for help or advice - but you have to ask.

The One Minute Networker will ask. It only takes a minute to pick up the phone and call someone in your network that can help you do whatever it is you need to do.

It comes as no surprise that men are always hesitant to ask directions, while women don't wait until they're already lost before seeking help. For some reason, men need to believe they can reach their destination by themselves; women just want to get there quickly.

The same is true in business. Sometimes you have to ask for directions: "Can you direct me to someone who knows about this" or "Do you know someone who could use my product or service?" If they can't help, perhaps they know someone who can. Ask: "Can you direct me to where I need to go?" Just make sure you know what you're asking for.

Have a clear definition of what you want from someone else. Ask for specific information, not generalities. A weak description will bring a generalized response that's not likely to be very useful.

There is another kind of direction to ask about, too. That's the direction your contact is going. We're all on our way somewhere, in transition from one condition to another. Circumstances continually change. Jobs are found or lost, children are born, children leave the nest, illness strikes, people are married or divorced - nothing remains the same forever. Here's a key: at transition points people are most open to change - you can offer that change.

Mindy Jones is a single mom in Georgia whose networking skills earn her a large six-figure income every year. She discovered early in her career that this kind of timing - transition — is everything.

"I listen to what people are saying," Mindy says. "I overhear conversations at the grocery store, at the park, in a movie line. I'm always looking for someone to talk to."

If you can find out what they're receptive to, where your new contacts want to go, there may be a way for you to help them get there. People will provide a wealth of information just in casual conversations if you're asking the right questions.

The right questions are those that elicit a response containing clues to the contact's thoughts and circumstances. In a non-threatening conversational style, interview for information. Make every question count. For example:

How's your family?

Here's where you can find out if a child is nearing college age (and if mom and dad have the money to pay for it), or if a younger family is bursting at the seams in a small house, and so on and so on. Maybe you can offer an opportunity for more income.

How is work and do you like what you do?

If you note some dissatisfaction here, you might be able to suggest an alternative. If the contact is happy with the job, maybe there is still interest in additional income. Is the employer utilizing the contact's leadership skills? If not, do you have a solution?

Is business going well?

Someone employed by a business that is facing hard times may well be more interested in your opportunity than someone with good prospects in a thriving business.

How's your health?

Someone in chronically poor health is probably looking for a way to continue earning an income after becoming unable to work a regular job. Maybe medical bills are the problem. Any ideas?

> **It's okay to ask for directions.**

Have you done any interesting traveling lately?

Let's say you learn that he/she would like to travel but can't afford it or doesn't have time. Perhaps you can help.

Obviously there are plenty of other questions. The point is that you want to find out everything you can about your contact because the more you know, the greater the possibility that you or someone in your network can fill that contact's needs at the very transitional moment they're most receptive to change. Be pleasantly persistent in getting the information, but get it.

Now you know how to ask for directions. Pick a specific goal you're currently working toward. Go to your list of people who've positively influenced you. Select one or two individuals from the list who can help you reach that goal. Call them and ask for help, advice or directions.

CONSTANT DRIPPING WILL WEAR AWAY
THE HARDEST STONE

LAW #5
Find 'em and File 'em

Jim Lindle, a former accountant who networked his way to great wealth, recalls that early in his career he was contemplating how to market a particular product he had acquired. Looking out the window of his hilltop house, Jim saw the neighborhood sprawled out below. Suddenly he thought, "Wow! Look at all of those people who need this product. And that's just one neighborhood. Think how big this can be!"

So, one by one, Jim began sharing what he had with his neighbors and friends. He had a simple approach: tell his neighbor about a new product he was now using, explain that it works and suggest that the neighbor try it. If the person liked the product, Jim simply asked if he/she would suggest it to friends. Many of them did, and Jim just kept doing it over and over until he became a multi-millionaire.

Like Jim, you can see all those people who need your service or your product. You just have to meet them - get them to open their eyes. My daughter plays a little game where she closes her eyes and believes that if she can't see me I can't see her. You know, in a way she's right.

Ask yourself this question: "How many people have I walked past today and didn't even make eye contact?" The One Minute Networker knows that when opportunity knocks you have to get off the couch and answer the door. It also doesn't hurt to open the door first, step outside and invite opportunity to come inside. How do you do that? Simply by meeting new people all of the time. Remember that people are looking for you. They need what you have to offer. They just don't know it yet.

I realize that very few of us are completely comfortable approaching a total stranger, but there are a couple of ways to make it easy enough that all of us can do it. Start by saying those "H" words: *Hi, Hello, How are you? How's it going?*

The singer Pink had a top five single titled "Let's Get This Party Started!" At the many conferences, parties, seminars and banquets I've attended over the years I've observed people who share this attitude. They mingle well and network like crazy, always saying the right thing to draw others out. I've also noticed that they all do the same thing when being introduced to someone new. Instead of saying just "Hello" or "Nice to meet you" or some similar greeting, they first repeat the person's name.

One Minute Networkers know that virtually all people love to hear their own name spoken. So after being introduced to Harry Potter, the One Minute Networker will respond with, "Hi, Harry Potter. I'm pleased to meet you. I'm ..." Because Harry likes to hear his own name he will appreciate it, and hearing yourself speak his name will help you remember it next time. As you say it, think of something to associate with the name to help you remember him.

Experts in memory improvement recommend that the more outrageous the association, the better you will remember the name. So, for example, you might create a mental image of Harry Potter as a flowerpot with hair - sort of a Chia pet.

If you're meeting someone without the benefit of a third-party introduction that tells you the name, start the conversation with your own. "Hi, I'm Oprah Winfrey. And you are...?" Now the person offers his name - James Bond — so your response is, "Nice to meet you, James Bond. And you're business is...?" It's easy, it breaks the ice, and it only takes one minute.

It also only takes one minute to make someone feel comfortable if you simply reflect his or her attitude and posture. If your contact speaks softly, reflect that back with a soft tone in your own voice. Someone more outgoing should find you outgoing and friendly as well. People are always more comfortable around those who are like themselves. Without being phony or transparent, sincerely be their reflection in the mirror when you first meet. It will give them confidence and build trust in you.

One of my friends, Richard Brooke, has built several very profitable businesses and earned a fortune in his career. Richard is a tremendous networker because every person he meets becomes a unique individual to him. He keeps a record of the person's name, the context in which they met, the person's occupation, and "...who is this person and what does he/she mean to me?" Richard maintains his information on Microsoft Outlook, but you can use anything from 3"x5" cards to a Palm Pilot or Blackberry. The key is to collect the kind of data about new people you meet that will be most useful and helpful to you.

Success isn't just a matter of who you know, but who you're willing to meet. Don't overlook the possibility that any or all of those individuals could bring a small miracle into your life. When you come in contact with others today, whether it's at the checkout stand, the bank line or the gas station, notice what's happening around you. Listen to what others are saying. Pay attention!

Observe and ask questions: Do you like being a bank teller? How long have you worked as a checker? How are the benefits at your job? Don't overlook an opportunity to add someone to your network just because you can't see a reason right away. Helping others and putting them into a better situation is an investment that will return great rewards in the long term.

Bob Snyder is a master of keeping in touch with others. He says, "It's pretty foolish to start building a relationship of trust and then just discard the prospect because the timing isn't right for them. So I drip on people - let them know what's happening and what they're missing out on. When their situation changes, they're ready to talk."

Bob "drips' simply by occasionally making a phone call or sending a note or an e-mail. He's not pressuring anyone, not making an overt sales pitch. But every call, note or whatever strengthens his connection to the contact/prospect. He's patient; he doesn't need an immediate reward or response.

Women understand this instinctively. My wife, Jackie, does things for others with no agenda, no need for a payback. You know many women like that. A woman says to her friend, "I'm starting a little business selling this. Will you host a party for me?" Without hesitation, the answer is, "Yes. Let's pick a date."

So they schedule the party, the friend rearranges her

schedule and plans some kind of refreshments. And it never occurs to her to ask, "What's in this for me?" She's just helping her friend get her business off the ground. She'll do all of this even if she has no interest in the product or getting into the business herself.

I've seen Jackie send out invitations, go shopping for fun food and get the house looking wonderful, all to help her friend. That's a great thing, because - trite as is sounds - what goes around comes around. There's no immediate benefit to Jackie for doing things for her friends, but in the long run, when she has a need somewhere down the line, her friends step up to help, no questions asked. They always do.

Our world is a huge web of people. By connecting some of them with each other, we also are connecting them to us. Remember "working the circle"? Every time you make one of these connections you become part of someone else's circle. Every time you create an opportunity for another person, other opportunities spin off and touch other lives that touch other lives. Eventually the connections and the opportunities find their way back to us.

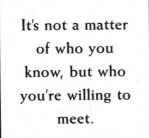

It's not a matter of who you know, but who you're willing to meet.

Now consider this: every time you add someone new to your circle, you add his or her entire circle to your network as well. It's been said that everyone can invite about 200 people to their wedding or their funeral. That's the number of friends, family and acquaintances each of us closely maintains over our lives. But what if you expanded that number by just two new people a week?

That's 104 new additions to your network every year. Well, that's not exactly accurate. Remember that each of those 104 new folks knows about 200 other people. So now you're potentially plugged into not 104 new people, but more than 20,000! See how simply this works? Your network grows exponentially very quickly!

Think about some of the good things that have happened in your life that seemed like pure luck or simple chance. Maybe it was finding the perfect house, or a friendship that changed your life. Perhaps it was "the big sale", if sales is your profession. Trace back through the sequence of events that resulted in these good things; they didn't just come out of nowhere. Something you did some time earlier, maybe even several years earlier - a phone call, a decision, a simple act - blossomed into a good thing later.

Jim Lindle says, "I believe inside of each one of us is a God-given potential to do really great things. There's something inside each one of us, something big, something important."

You can do one simple thing today that will grow into something amazing days or months from now!

Decide to meet five new individuals this week. Remember that you have to get enough information about them to add to your newly expanding file of network contacts: name, phone number, e-mail address and occupation. And make a unique note to help remember them. For example, the Dale Earnhart #3 decal in a new contact's car window means he's a NASCAR fan. Whether you also like auto racing doesn't matter; you now know something about your contact that can be useful later.

Guess what? Now you're networking!

IF PEOPLE DON'T KNOW YOU'RE IN BUSINESS, YOU'RE NOT IN BUSINESS

– BARRY DONALDSON

LAW #6
Top Of The Mind

Once on a business trip I sat next to a fascinating man during the flight. He had a very successful billboard business. He told me about how he had started it by buying just a single billboard. Then he bought a second one, then another. By the time I met him, he owned a network of billboards throughout Texas, Missouri and several other states; he was worth a fortune.

He told me the secret to success in business is "top of the mind." What he meant was this: because of your efforts to spread your message, when a prospect needs your service or product, your name should be the first one that comes up. You are at the "top of the mind."

A 30-second spot advertisement during the Superbowl costs about $2.5 million! Companies are willing to pay that astounding rate because, given the audience for that broadcast, it's worth it. What's your message worth? Given your own potential, it could be worth more than a Superbowl spot.

Remember, if people don't know you're in business, you're not in business. So whether it's for your business or for you personally, you need to develop your own "commercial." To the people you meet and associate with today, you are your own billboard, radio spot and TV ad. The message you project should be as carefully planned as any company's advertising campaign to place you at the "top of the mind."

We've all been to parties or get-togethers of some kind where we meet new people. We stand around making small talk. Sometimes we make a useful contact; sometimes we don't. We can change those odds.

How do you usually greet someone you've not seen in some time? You probably ask, "What's new?" It's a formality; a detailed answer is not expected. The response you're most likely to get is "Not much." This also is just a formality; the other person doesn't believe that you really want to know anyway. But that's absolutely the wrong answer for the effective networker to give. Imagine the opportunities you will create if you're prepared with a real answer, one that generates - even requires - a response to you.

For example, I was at an industry conference when someone looked at my tag with my company's name on it.

"Dream Builders?" she asked. "What's that?"

Usually when I've been asked that question I've had a 2-3 minute answer, but this time I simply said, "We keep people up at night." With an inquisitive smile, she asked what I meant by that. I didn't launch into a long detailed explanation. I just answered her question with a question, "You know how companies use DVDs and CD ROMs to get their message out to the public?"

She said yes. So I added, "We produce those DVDs and CD ROMs, and we do such a good job for companies like yours that people are up all night thinking about your business."

It was a technique I learned from Hilton Johnson. He teaches people how to keep a conversation going with someone you have just met. After your "billboard" message has attracted the other person's attention and he or she has asked more about it, Hilton suggests that you answer the question with a question, such as: "You know how people are looking for (name your subject)?" The contact will say, "Yes." That's your opening to continue, "Well, that's what we do." You get the picture.

In the past I've always responded to a question like this woman's with some lengthy explanation about my company's services. But my brief direct answer got her attention. It doesn't seem like much, but she left that conference thinking about my business.

If I say that same thing to enough people, here and there in my daily routine, soon I'll have built a network of billboards promoting my message. What does it cost me?

Nothing. What's the payoff? Now there are hundreds of people out there saying Dream Builders keeps people up at night. Cowboy philosopher Will Rogers was right when he said, "Get someone else to toot your horn and it will travel twice as far."

At least 20 people should have seen or heard your "commercial" in the last week. That's the minimum number you must reach in order to create the lifestyle change you want, with plenty of time freedom and financial security. Just as with any national advertising campaign by a major corporation, the success of your commercial depends to a great extent on "frequency." The more often people hear or see your message, the more effective it (and you) will be.

Advertising professionals agree that the most effective message should be short, to the point and it must appeal to an emotion. Clearly explain enough of what you do that your listener will understand, and have a "hook" that will make them want to know more. Most of all, you want them to remember and tell others about you.

When I said, "We keep people up at night" I met each of the advertising criteria. It is a short response, it is very direct and it makes the listener want to know more by appealing to his/her curiosity. We're now a "sound bite" society. Keep your message in that context, brief and to the point. Remember, your "personal commercial" is the only opportunity you'll get to make a first impression.

Another reason for having a snappy, memorable way to describe what you do is that you get to hear yourself say it again and again. By that I mean that every time you sell it or tell it, your belief system is reinforced. Drew Earl has trained hundreds of thousands of people to believe in themselves and their products. He says strong beliefs are like anesthetic: they help take away the pain of rejection. Every time you hear a description of your business or profession you have another opportunity to say to yourself, "Yeah, that's why I love my product or my service. This is why I love what I do." It's a powerful subconscious thing that happens.

The key is to take advantage of every opportunity even if you can't see an immediate gain. Live in the moment — right now, today. Have you ever had an eye exam? Remember how the optometrist sat you in the chair and made you peer through that machine that looked like binoculars on steroids? He took you from lens to lens gradually until he found the combination you needed. Is this better or is this better? Sometimes during that process you couldn't tell the difference between lens "A" and lens "B." Opportunity is like that. Every new opportunity will eventually become visible, but you can't force it.

> "Get someone else to toot your horn and it will travel twice as far."

Reflecting on his long working relationship with the late Johnny Carson, bandleader Doc Severinson said the late-night host's phenomenal success came because he never forced a situation. He never tried to make things happen, Doc explained. He just let them happen.

When you write your "commercial" don't use the computer. Take an old-fashioned sheet of paper and a pencil with an eraser to a quiet place where you can think. Write an accurate description of what you do.

Don't give up if your commercial doesn't just fall off the end of the pencil onto the paper. Simple and brief as they are, "Built Ford Tough" and Little Caesar's "Pizza, Pizza" weren't a professional copywriter's first attempt, either.

Take as long as you like. Let it happen. But after you have written your masterpiece, take the eraser and start cutting it down to 15 words or less. The result will be a great conversation starter.

If you want a "billboard" similar to "We keep people up at night", keep erasing until you have only 6 - 7 words.

Now you're networking again.

SEND OUT WHAT YOU WISH
TO ATTRACT

LAW #7
Casting Your Net

When I was a boy I played baseball. One day when I
was about nine years old my dad and I were walking home
after a game and one of my teammates was walking part of
the way with us. All the way to his house this boy talked
about what a great game he had played that day. He went
on and on about how well he hit the ball and what a great
fielder he was. I was getting into the spirit of it a little
myself, reinforcing what he was saying.

After we dropped my friend off at his house, we walked
a little farther and my dad stopped. He said, "I don't like
how that boy kept talking about himself."

Well, my father was pretty old school, very reserved. He
was a southern gentleman from North Carolina, a man of
few words. So when he said that about my teammate I took
it to mean that I was not to talk about myself. It's boastful,
it's bragging and it annoys people.

So for a long time after that I took it to the extreme. I

would never share my successes or talk about them. It seemed wrong to do that. Lots of people feel that way, too, especially about sharing their business or products. But One Minute Networkers love to pass on good news. They want to be the first to tell you when they find a good thing. They love what they do; they believe in it so much they feel an obligation to share it. They're excited, and it shows in what they say and how they say it. The One Minute Networker is a natural self-promoter. I don't mean the boastful, backslapping kind of self-promotion, but the confident, sincere approach that gathers all kinds of people in your net.

That's the difference between boasting and casting a net. Boasting or bragging is self-centered; it's about me and what I've done or what I have. Casting a net is focused on others, on sharing a good thing with someone else, even a stranger.

Whether you sell a product or provide a service you must personally believe it is the very best product or the most useful service in the world. You can't live without it and no one else should either. This is a breakthrough moment when you realize that you want to share what you have regardless of whether there is anything to gain. When you are your own best customer, your enthusiasm will show through in the smile on your face.

I love people who can smile. Driving my car one day I smiled at someone and, at the same time, saw my face in the rear view mirror - there was no smile. I felt like I was smiling, but the feeling apparently wasn't getting through to my face. I wasn't projecting the image I thought I was. What do people actually see when you smile at them? A smile catches everyone's attention; it's the easiest way in the world to get noticed.

Too many of us hold back because we don't want to seem overbearing. Some of us don't realize that there is a polite, or an appropriate, way to share what you have. In our desire to not push we sometimes fall into the "just" trap. You know, we'll phone a contact and say, "It's just me, calling to..." Or maybe it's "I'm just following up on..." Remember, the word "just" is a clear signal that what you're about to say isn't that important. Don't make that mistake.

Find a comfortable balance between aggressive and timid. It will take a little experimentation to find what works best, especially because everyone you meet is different. Practice until you get better at it. When you approach someone in a way that's natural to you and appropriate to the other person, you're casting your net into fruitful waters.

I like to begin every day with a "call-out" session, a time set aside for making phone calls to some of those in my network who might help me or whom I might be able to serve. I'm reaching out to people, making contact, keeping in touch. This list will change regularly, depending upon what I'm doing. Your call-out list will do the same. Whether it takes 15 minutes or an hour to make those calls, do it without fail.

Of course, you're not likely to reach everyone on your list. You will be leaving messages - voicemail or answering machines - for some of them. That message could be a "Thought to Live By", a joke or anything they'll find interesting that stands apart from other messages on their machine. By doing that you are "filling the pipeline," giving others a reason to contact you. You're ensuring a certain percentage of callbacks. Do this religiously every day and you will never run out of contacts.

Earlier I suggested that you make a "no strings" phone call to someone whose name pops into your mind for whatever reason. It's important. But this daily call-out session is the place to make some calls with strings attached. That is, make set-up calls that allow you to present your opportunity or product by gently challenging your contact's status quo.

Here's how you do that. Choose someone whose circumstances you're familiar with - job, approximate income level, family size, etc. Call that person today and say simply, "Tom (or Kim), I've been thinking about you and I believe you're worth a lot more than you're getting paid right now." Doing nothing more than making this simple comment accomplishes several good things.

1. It lets Kim know that someone else has been thinking about her. That makes her feel good.

2. It says that someone else has been thinking the same thing Kim has been thinking all along: "I'm worth more than my employer is paying me. I have more to offer than this."

3. When you drop that comment "out of the blue" you absolutely guarantee that Kim will respond in a way that opens the door to your offer/product/service/opportunity. No one can ignore that kind of sincere compliment. No one.

I know a man who specializes in taking private companies public all across the nation and does very well at it. One reason he succeeds is that he makes himself memorable to everyone he meets. His favorite tool is a simple stick of gum. No matter where you meet him, or when, he'll offer you a stick of chewing gum. He carries packs of the stuff in nearly every flavor; he buys it by the gross. When he offers the gum he presents it like a fan, or a hand of playing cards. Every time I see him I have to laugh because I know he's going to bring out that gum. It's become his signature, and people remember him.

I'm not suggesting that you carry chewing gum with you. While that works for my friend, it isn't for everyone. But you should condition yourself to choose some little thing that will cause people to remember you. It can be anything.

In my business I regularly use "voice-over" professionals. These are the actors you never see, but whose voices you hear on television commercials and other video productions. One of these "talents", as they're called, once or twice a year sends me a little gift, some kind of gadget. It might be a calculator or a pen with something goofy on it. What the gift is doesn't matter; that he sends it for no particular reason does matter.

I have a desk calendar with clever cartoon artwork on it. Whenever I come across a cartoon that reminds me of someone in particular, I copy it, write a note and fax or mail it to the person. It's just another way to be at the "top of the mind" by renewing the contact.

You can do the same thing. It doesn't have to be anything expensive. Maybe it's a bottle of purified water with your business card attached. Maybe it's nothing more than a handwritten note or a greeting card. Anything that reminds someone of you and your business will do. But get into the habit of giving small innocent gifts.

Mike McDonald is a phenomenally successful networker in Texas. He credits part of that success to his habit of maintaining contact with people, even if they aren't interested in his opportunity at the time. Periodically he checks back with a brief phone call or a card in the mail. One time, while enjoying the winter sun in the Caribbean, he bought postcards picturing the beach and his luxury hotel. He mailed them to some of those contacts with a simple message: "Having a great time. Wish you were here." That's a powerful message and incentive that cost Mike practically nothing and took only one minute to do.

I love to send greeting cards. When I learn about someone's birthday or achievement - maybe in casual conversations — I'll find an appropriate card and send it right then.

Notice my preference for actual, physical cards sent by snail mail. Now there is even an Internet service that sends cards for me personalized with a note and signature in my own handwriting! Don't get me wrong; I communicate in my business every day through e-mail. It's an incredibly valuable tool, but I use it to communicate information, not to connect with people. Connecting is better done with a card or a letter. Everyone likes to get mail. It's much more personal. So is a phone call. There simply is no substitute for a personal, one-on-one conversation to make or renew a connection with someone.

Something else that's just as important as "top of the mind" is by giving these cards, I'm living in abundance. I'm sending out the good feelings that I want to attract.

This goes back to the idea that sometimes we do something good for others without requiring anything of them in return. A neighbor mentions that his car is running a little rough, so you give him the name of the mechanic or service center where you have your vehicles maintained. In the course of the conversation you both chitchat about your families, Saturday chores and work - you make sure he knows your line of business. Sometime later that neighbor is visiting with his brother-in-law, Bob, who says he needs to find someone who does what you do. Your neighbor says, "Hey, Bob, the guy across the street does that. Why not give him a call?" Sound familiar?

Here's an example of doing a good thing just because it is the right thing. It's also evidence that doing something good in the face of a negative experience can erase the negative and keep you from slipping out of abundance. I recently was faced with writing a letter to a new client in which I had to clear up a misunderstanding while still striving to maintain our good relationship. I wasn't looking forward to doing it.

So, while driving to work on the day I planned to write the letter, I stopped to get bagels for everyone at the office. This was a good way to begin my day on a positive note.

Time was short so the drive-through window seemed like a good choice. I was just turning into the drive-up lane when another driver cut in front of me. My first thought was, "Oh, great! I have to write this letter I don't want to write, I'm running late and now this guy cuts me off. This is not a good start to my day."

I turned out of the drive-up lane, intending to just go to the office with a foul attitude and no bagels. Then I changed my mind. My friends at the office would enjoy the bagels even if I didn't. So I parked my car, now intending to make my purchase inside at the counter. As I opened my door I heard a car alarm screeching further out in the parking lot.

It was coming from a car with an obviously flustered grandmotherly woman standing beside it, fumbling with her keys. So I drove over, parked my car and got out to see if I could help. The alarm was deafening, but after unsuccessfully trying every possible way to stop the noise, I decided that it could only be shut off after the car was started. I helped the woman into the car so she could do that, but she was still so flustered by the noise that she wasn't able to fit the key into the ignition. Finally I reached through the window across her (she told me I smelled good), started the car and turned off the alarm. The sudden silence was beautiful.

I cautioned her that the alarm was likely to go off again at random until it was fixed. She thanked me for my help and drove away. I bought some bagels and drove to my office to face the dreaded letter-writing task. But now, somehow, it was no longer something to fear. My mood had changed because I had done something good for someone already that morning. I felt good again. Feeling good is important because when you feel good you find the real you. And when you find the real you, exciting and impressive things begin to happen.

Incidentally, that letter I was dreading was never written. The client called me and we resolved the questions over the phone. That felt good, too.

There's a secret to feeling good. It's called "service." Whether it's a big thing or something small like helping the woman with her car alarm, it works every time, in two ways. First, if you can find a way to serve someone else, that person will become a viable part of your network. Second, service puts you "in the spirit" to succeed; you're "inspired."

Unlike motivation, which can fade, inspiration is internal. Since inspiration has no limits, neither do you!

Another simple thing I do has been a gold mine over the years. No one likes to feel rejected, but the reality is that you're going to be rejected more times than you're accepted. Don't let it bother you. Theodore Geisel, author of the Dr. Seuss books, was rejected 29 times before a publisher gave him a chance. Michael Jordan was cut from his high school basketball team. The first year sales of Coca Cola totaled little more than 400 bottles.

When I've been turned down on an offer or not been selected for a bid it feels a lot like rejection. Well, okay, it is rejection. But I don't take it personally; they didn't reject me and who I am. It was only my proposal that wasn't accepted. They are not the same, and recognizing that fact makes all the difference in the world in my attitude.

So I send the contact a "maybe next time" note. It just says thanks for meeting with me, or considering my offer or whatever it was, and I wish the contact well and a "maybe next time." With most people, there will be another opportunity to work together. Because of my note I'll be at the "top of the mind" when another project comes up, and I'll get that call. This is another aspect of casting my net. Get in the habit of sending "maybe next time" notes. It costs practically nothing and pays well over the long haul.

There's another reason I send that note: because it makes me feel good in the face of something negative. I always want to feel good. Don't you? My mother is one of those rare people who is always "up" and cheerful. When I was little she didn't just talk, she would "sing-talk." You know what that is - ♪♪Bryyyyaaan. Time to get uuuuuup!♪♪ — like she's singing. She feels good doing that. It's hard to sing and feel bad at the same time. I've always wondered if she sings because she's happy or if she's happy because she sings. Either way, it's also pretty difficult to hear someone sing and still feel bad (except for my grandmother, who might say of someone's singing, "Kill it. Don't let it suffer."), so hearing Mom sing-talk makes me feel as good as she does. Most of us are not naturally that positive all of the time, but everything would go much better if we tried to be that way.

> **"Service puts you 'in the spirit' to succeed."**

So send someone a card or give him or her a phone call. Tell this person you appreciate the example he or she has set for you. Ask for nothing. Simply send out what you wish to attract - and wait patiently.

IF WE CHANGE THE WAY WE LOOK AT THINGS, THE THINGS WE LOOK AT CHANGE

– DR. WAYNE DYER

LAW #8
Same Play

When I was young my friends and I loved to meet after school to play football on the field of our elementary school. Good weather or bad, it didn't matter. We simply needed an excuse to get dirty and feel like men. None of us went on to be high school or college star players, but we loved to play the game.

We especially liked when one of the guys would come up with some dazzling hand-off pass play. Many times I returned to the huddle to report that "the man covering me was too slow and I was wide open." Whoever was quarterbacking at the time would listen to my report and everyone else's. Then he would utter those two words only a battlefield commander could speak: "Same play."

Same play? Yes. It meant that each of us was to do exactly what we had done on the last play. But now all the quarterback had to do was throw the ball to someone else, someone he hadn't seen open before. This time the same play gained more yardage. It worked every time.

Many of us think we have to come up with some new play every day, week or month. We falsely believe that we have to reinvent ourselves to do better in our businesses. But the truth is that we just need some minor adjustments and more practice. Self-help guru Dr. Wayne Dyer says that if we change the way we look at things, the things we look at change. Same play; just see who else in your life is open and move the ball forward.

Calvin Coolidge put it this way:
"Nothing in the world can take the place of persistence. Talent will not; nothing is more common than unsuccessful men with talent. Genius will not; unrewarded genius is almost a proverb. Education will not; the world is full of educated derelicts. Persistence and determination alone are omnipotent."

Persistence and determination are easier to sustain if you follow a consistent routine. Discipline is simply remembering what you want. Self-discipline just might be the most critical factor in any kind of success or achievement, and self-discipline is created by routine. Now before you tell me that routine bores you, consider the freedom that a disciplined routine offers.

Following an established routine that you have prioritized keeps you organized. Being organized means you don't have to waste time rushing here and there putting out fires; you have time to concentrate on more important things. Develop a routine that allows you to use your time most efficiently. A routine also means that you don't have to reinvent any wheels.

There are plenty of very talented people out there who will never reach their potential because they spend too much time trying to improve things that don't need improvement. Of course we should all be creative and innovative - those are common traits of entrepreneurs - but that energy shouldn't be wasted simply because we don't want to follow those who blazed the trail ahead of us.

Chances are your company or organization already has studied the market, developed the training, created the sales tools, made the mistakes and corrected them, so all you have to do is plug that information into your daily and weekly routines and get going. Take advantage of all of that free expertise and proven tools to make yourself more productive.

Keep talking to people. Standing silently on the sidelines watching others play the game won't get you any closer to your own goals. I promise that if you stick with your game plan and keep looking for the open man, you will have and be what you dream about.

I have a friend, Mitch Huhem, who is a remarkable networker and businessman. Ask him to tell you his secret and he quickly says "WIN". I know, I know, that's too simple. But there's more to it. WIN is an acronym for What's Important Now. According to Mitch, "There really are only one or two things we do that make up most of the difference in our lives."

It's like the "80/20 Rule of Organizations." In most sales organizations you'll find that 80% of the volume usually comes from 20% of the people. The same ratio seems to be true when it comes to our individual income-producing activities. We can waste our time trying new campaigns and approaches month after month, **but what we focus on is what prospers.**

I believe that when most people get sidetracked from their dreams and goals it is self-induced distraction. Winning can be just as frightening to some as losing. Internationally acclaimed author and lecturer, Marianne Williamson, said it best in her book A Return to Love: "Our greatest fear is not that we are inadequate. Our deepest fear is that we are powerful beyond measure. It is our light, not our darkness, that most frightens us..."

> **"Discipline is remembering what you want."**

Whenever you get into a rut and feel like you're spinning your wheels, ask yourself, "What's important now?" Is it checking your emails? Is it leaving your desk to do something else? Or is it making those phone calls you've been putting off?

Take a minute to look at your day and compare it with your schedule, continually reevaluating. Commit your daily task list to paper, so you have it constantly in front of you. This will help you be more productive by staying on task and not wasting your time doing busy work. Begin doing the most important things first.

When she was ten years old my eldest daughter, Micah, said, "Dad, everything begins with a try." She could have added that every failure begins by doing nothing. If you continually do what's important now, you'll end your day with much more accomplished.

∞∞∞

NOTHING IS AS REAL AS A DREAM. THE WORLD CAN CHANGE AROUND YOU BUT YOUR DREAM WILL NOT

–TOM CLANCY

LAW #9
Expect Miracles

Several years ago I was very busy building a large sales organization. In the midst of all that intense activity we were remodeling our house and I needed a plumber. On the freeway one day I passed an old, rusting pickup truck with a faded sign advertising the driver as a plumber. On the spot, I called the number on the truck and arranged for the work to be done. While he was working we chatted about his business. He completed the repair and went on his way.

A couple of years later I saw him again. This time he was not driving a rusty old truck; he was now behind the wheel of a sleek jet-black Jaguar. Turned out that he never had liked plumbing and had been looking for an opportunity at the time I met him. Someone gave him one (not me - I had looked right past him!) and he discovered that he was a natural networker. His sales organization and the volume it generated were phenomenal. At a time when I was focused specifically on building a committed sales organization I had allowed the old truck and the plumber's tools to cloud my judgment of this man. The plumber expected a miracle and got it to the tune of about $12M; I got a lesson in missed opportunities.

The most successful networkers understand that their networks can be set in motion to help them reach their goals, so they expect miracles to happen to them. Duncan MacDonald, down in Texas, is a great example. Just over three years ago he was broke, quite literally living out of his car. He kept a small file cabinet in the trunk; he used the $3 showers at truck stops because he couldn't afford even cheap motel rooms. But he had a dream, he believed in himself and he refused to give up.

"I knew for a fact that, whatever my present circumstances, it would happen. I would be wealthy," he says, looking back on his odyssey from scarcity to abundance. That's expecting a miracle. And he got it. Today he leads a large business organization and makes well over a million dollars a year!

While you have to have lofty long-term goals, don't overlook those smaller opportunities at your feet today. There is a story about a Pennsylvania farmer in the early 1900s who decided to sell his farm and go to work for his cousin in the oil business in Canada. But the cousin turned him down because the farmer knew nothing about oil.

So the farmer began to study the oil business. He read everything he could find about how to find oil, how to process it, how to determine its type and uses. He became an expert. Now his cousin agreed to hire him. The farmer sold his farm and left for Canada to join his cousin.

The new owner of the farm, while watering cattle one day, discovered that the previous owner had put a plank in the stream to divert an oily scum that continually built up near the stream banks. As it turned out, the farmer who had spent all of that time studying oil had overlooked the presence on his own property of oil that was eventually valued at about $100 million! He had sold his farm for just $833.

Just as we shouldn't look past opportunities at our feet, we also cannot afford to give up too soon on any of them. We all hit those lulls when we feel bogged down. But as my ever-optimistic friend Mark Ludwig, whose clients include half of the Fortune 100, says, "Everything we do is difficult in the middle." The trick is to force ourselves into action so we can get past the middle to the success that is waiting on the far side.

The "what if" factor holds great power for fighting the urge to give up. Make it an integral part of everything you do. Let's say you sell a product that a number of other companies also sell. Mr. Jones will decide at some point to make a large purchase, but a number of salespeople will call on him before he says yes. You can go see Mr. Jones with your head down, assuming that he's not ready yet to decide. Or you can say "what if?" "What if I'm the one he's waiting for? What if it's me?"

Now reinforce that. Is there any good reason to believe you're not the one Jones is waiting to meet? Of course not. Is there every reason to believe you are it? Certainly there is. Expect the miracle. Miracles are everywhere. The trick is to see them.

Even though our natural instinct is to see what we can get out of this now, the One Minute Networker knows and understands that giving without expecting an immediate return will one day pay big dividends. It's all about timing. It's patience, and understanding that every good act has multiple rewards. But they may not come around next week or even next month.

A stonecutter may have to strike the stone with his hammer a hundred times before the 101st blow splits the stone. That final blow can only be successful because of all those that preceded it. The stonecutter can teach us two things. He doesn't know in advance how many blows it will take to split the stone; each stone is different. He does know, however, that if he doesn't quit too soon, any stone can be cut.

Networking is very much like stonecutting. At first all you can see is the huge rock. You can't know in advance how many contacts you will have to make or how many meetings you will have to attend before the chisel finally cleaves the stone. But you can know that if you keep making those connections - doing the basics over and over - you will succeed. The stone will split for you. Expect the miracle, plan for the miracle, and watch the miracle happen.

The toughest part of networking just might be accepting the fact that it isn't always about you. Remember Mr. Straw? Not one of his "trades" was made consciously to make him wealthy. But every one of his trades, done out of concern for someone else's needs, moved him a little closer to the wealth he ultimately enjoyed. We all can be like Mr. Straw - with the same results - if we learn to help others instead of only ourselves.

Within these pages you have learned a number of things you can do to succeed in whatever you're doing, things that will simplify your life and make it better. None of them take very long; most take one minute, none are difficult. But I promise you that if you incorporate only one of them into your daily comings and goings it will be a life-changing experience. I can say that because I've done it and because I have personally seen others do it.

The next 60 seconds are yours. They are always yours.

> **Miracles are everywhere. The trick is to see them.**

The only way to determine where you will be next week, next year or twenty years from now is to decide what to do with the one minute facing you right now. Hours and days will be productive only when the minutes within them are wisely used. Do the right thing. Be a One Minute Networker!

After you have applied what you have learned from this book and have begun to enjoy the benefits that come to you, take a minute to share your experience with me. I'm serious - send me an e-mail relating how the book has helped you. I'm especially interested in networking stories you and I can share with others.

Send me an e-mail at bryan@theoneminutenetworker.com

Special thanks, to my mom, who still sing-talks to make people happy.

About the Author

Bryan Thayer's love for networking began in childhood and has never waned. He is thrilled by challenge and lives for achieving his end goal.

He has built a marketing organization of several thousand sales representatives for an international corporation. He is now president of his own successful, full-service multimedia company.

A popular and sought-after speaker, Bryan has shared his networking ideas at conventions and motivational seminars across the country. He admits to being a dreamer at heart, and he most enjoys finding ways to help other people make their own ideas a reality.

Bryan and his wife, Jackie, have four children and live in Utah.

Get More Valuable Networking Tips -- FREE!

Subscribe to Bryan Thayer's free online video newsletter, The Networking Minute, and you'll receive valuable tips and ideas each week on how to continue improving your networking skills.

To subscribe now, go to:
http://www.thenetworkingminute.com

Get the Audio Book Version of The One Minute Networker

Maximize your networking skills by listening to the audio book version of The One Minute Networker no matter where you are! This high fidelity recording is read by the author Bryan Thayer.

Order your copy now at:
http://www.theoneminutenetworker.com/audiobook

Have Bryan Thayer Speak At Your Next Event

Looking for someone exciting and different to speak to your organization? Let Bryan Thayer energize your group with his fun and innovative ways of motivating people to achieve greater success.

For more information, go to:
http://www.theoneminutenetworker.com/speaking